Highlights

PRESCHOOL

AGES 3–5

Hands-On STEAM
Learning Fun Workbook

For information about permission to reproduce selections from this book for
an entire school or school district, please contact permissions@highlights.com.

Published by Highlights Learning • 815 Church Street • Honesdale, Pennsylvania 18431
ISBN: 978-1-64472-186-5
Mfg. 07/2020
Printed in Brainerd, MN, USA
First edition
10 9 8 7 6 5 4 3 2 1

For assistance in the preparation of this book, the editors would like to thank:
Vanessa Maldonado, MSEd; MS Literacy Ed. K–12; Reading/LA Consultant Cert.; K–5 Literacy Instructional Coach
Kristin Ward, MS Curriculum, Instruction, and Assessment; K–5 Mathematics Instructional Coach
Jump Start Press, Inc.

The Four Seasons

Draw a picture to show each season. Then, draw lines to match each season with an object on the right.

Fall

Winter

Spring

Summer

TALK ABOUT IT!

What is the weather like in each season where you live? Which season is the coldest? Which season is the warmest?

What Should You Wear?

Use a **red** crayon to color each warm-weather item.

Use a **blue** crayon to color each cold-weather item.

The words hot, sunny, snowy, and cold tell about weather. Use what you know about the weather to choose what to wear.

Circle the differences you see in these rainy-day pictures.

TALK ABOUT IT!

What are the children in the photos wearing?
Why do you think they dress like this on a rainy day?

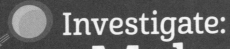
Make a Wind Gauge

YOU NEED:
- a ribbon or string
- a stick

1. With an adult's help, tie the ribbon or string to one end of the stick.

2. Take the wind gauge outside. Look at what happens to the ribbon. How does this help you understand how hard the wind is blowing?

Wind is moving air. You can't see wind, but you can see how it affects objects.

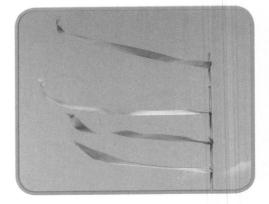

Draw a line between each kite and its exact match.

Cloudy Day

Look at each picture. Circle the clouds that are a sign of fair weather. Draw an **X** on the clouds that mean a storm is coming.

On fair, or calm, days, clouds are white and fluffy. When a storm is coming, clouds look dark and heavy.

Sometimes people think clouds look like other shapes. What do these clouds look like?

TALK ABOUT IT!

Go outside and look at the sky. Do you see any clouds? What kinds of shapes do they make?

Investigate:
Give a Weather Report

YOU NEED:
- drawing paper
- crayons or markers

1. Observe the weather every day for one week. Draw a weather picture each day. Label the picture with the date.

2. At the end of the week, look at each picture you drew.

3. Report on what the weather was like during the week.

TALK ABOUT IT!
How many days were sunny? How many days were cloudy? Did it rain? What else did you notice about the week's weather?

Push or Pull?

These children are moving a wagon. Which one is pulling the wagon? Which child is pushing it?

A push moves an object away from you. A pull moves an object toward you.

Each child below is pushing something. In what direction will the object go? Draw an arrow to show the direction.

TALK ABOUT IT!

What is something that you can pull? How would it move when you pull it?

Investigate:
Magnetic Pulls

YOU NEED:

• a magnet
• objects to test, such as a crayon, paper clip, glue stick, nail, and playing card

The force of a magnet **attracts** some metal objects. It pulls the objects toward itself.

1. Look at the objects. Predict. Which ones will a magnet attract?

2. Hold the magnet near each object.

3. Complete the chart. Put a ✓ in the correct column to show whether the magnet attracts the object.

4. Draw another item to test in the bottom row. Test it.

Object	Yes	No

TALK ABOUT IT!

Which objects did the magnet attract? What happened? Which objects were not attracted? How do you know?

Push and Pull Fun

An object that is heavier needs more force to move it.

Color the wagon that would be harder to pull.

You want to push a ball toward this block tower to knock it down. Circle the ball you should use.

TALK ABOUT IT!

Which wagon did you color? Why?

Which ball did you circle? Why?

 Invent:

Make a Vehicle

Build any vehicle you can imagine. Give it wheels to make it move.

YOU NEED:
- materials to make wheels, such as cardboard circles or play dough
- materials to make axles, such as straws or pencils
- materials for a base, such as a paper-towel tube or tissue box
- glue • paint or markers
- scissors

NOTE: You may need to ask an adult to cut holes in the wheels to fit in axles.

1. Choose some round objects for the wheels.

2. Wheels need to turn on rods called *axles*. Put one wheel onto an axle. Then, add another wheel on the other end of the axle. If you want a 4-wheel vehicle, make another set of wheels and an axle.

3. Add a base. Attach it to the axles. Be sure the wheels can still turn.

4. Decorate your vehicle with paint or markers.

5. Take your invention for a test drive!

TALK ABOUT IT!
How well does your invention work? What could you change to make it better?

Photography: Andrea Killam

 **Invent:**

Build a Ramp

Test ideas to see how far a toy car can move.

YOU NEED:
- blocks or heavy books
- small toy car • tape

The height of a ramp affects how fast and far an object moves.

1. Use blocks or books to build a ramp.
2. Place the car at the top of the ramp. Let go.
3. How far does the car go? Place a piece of tape on the floor where it stops.
4. Add or remove blocks to change the height of the ramp.
5. Repeat steps 2 and 3. How far does the car go now?

TALK ABOUT IT!

How far does the car go each time? Is there a change? Why do you think this happens?
Does the type of car matter? Test different ones.

 Invent:
Make a Boat to Float!

What can you invent and build that will float in water? Build anything you can imagine and see if it floats.

YOU NEED:
- materials to make the base, such as craft sticks or wax cartons • large tub half full of water • glue
- construction paper, paint, or markers • scissors

1. Gather materials to make your base. Test them in the tub or small stream with an adult to see whether they float. Choose the ones that float best.

2. Decorate your base any way you would like. Add some walls or a sail.

3. Test your invention. Does it still float?

TALK ABOUT IT!

How well does your invention work? What could you change to make it better?

Photography: Andrea Killam

Solid or Liquid?

Think about pouring milk into a bowl of cereal. The bowl and cereal are solids. The milk is liquid.

A solid keeps its shape. A liquid flows and takes the shape of its container.

Look at the objects below. Circle each liquid. Draw an X on each solid.

TALK ABOUT IT!

How can you tell whether something is solid or liquid? Look around your home. What solids and liquids can you find?

Liquids and Solids

Some water is liquid. But this water is solid. Solid water is ice.

When you freeze liquid water it becomes solid. When you add heat to ice, the ice melts, or changes back to liquid water.

Draw a line to match each solid to its liquid form.

TALK ABOUT IT!

Compare each solid to its liquid form. How are they the same? How are they different?

On the Ice

Find and circle the **8** objects in this Hidden Pictures puzzle.

envelope

magnifying glass

sailboat

needle

crown

arrow

candle

open book

TALK ABOUT IT!

Which objects in the picture are solids? What liquids do you see? How can you tell the difference?

Investigate:
Make Frozen Hot Cocoa

Turn a hot liquid into a frozen solid.

YOU NEED:

• hot cocoa   • mini marshmallows (optional)   • ice-pop molds

1. Make hot cocoa. Have an adult help you. Add marshmallows, if you want. Set aside the cocoa to cool.

2. Pour the cocoa into the ice-pop molds. If you don't have ice-pop molds, you can use an ice-cube tray. Cover the tray with plastic wrap and stick a toothpick in each cube section.

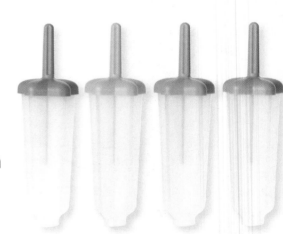

3. Place the pops in the freezer. When they are frozen, remove them and enjoy!

TALK ABOUT IT!

How does changing the temperature affect the cocoa? How do you know?

Morning and Night

These pictures show day and night.

TALK ABOUT IT!

What does the girl see in the daytime sky?
What does she see in the nighttime sky?

Draw something you do during the day. Then draw something you do at night. Include the sky in each picture.

Day	Night

Day or Night?

Look at each picture. Color the sun if the picture shows daytime. Color the moon if the picture shows nighttime.

TALK ABOUT IT!

Which pictures show daytime? Which ones show nighttime? How do you know?

Moon Watching

Does the moon always look the same? How much of the moon we can see changes each day.

This poem describes 3 moon shapes.

Full moon
Gray balloon
Bobbing in the sky
It got away
In the day
And now it's
flying high

Moon half
Like a laugh
In a starry face
A crooked smile
Crossing miles
Of inky outer
space

Crescent moon
Shiny spoon
Stirring up the night
Or cookie round
That was found
And eaten bite
by bite

Look at each moon shape in the top row. Point to its match in the bottom row.

TALK ABOUT IT!
Look at the sky tonight. Can you see the moon? What does it look like?

Create:
A Constellation

A star gives off light. A group of stars in a pattern is called a constellation.

YOU NEED:
- rocks
- white, black, and glow-in-the-dark paint
- paintbrush

1. Wash and dry your rocks.

2. Paint white stars on the top of your rocks. Let them dry.

3. Paint the stars with glow-in-the-dark paint. Let them dry.

4. Paint the areas around the stars black. Let them dry.

5. Place your rocks in a sunny spot. Arrange the rocks to make your constellation. The stars will soak up the light during the day and glow at night.

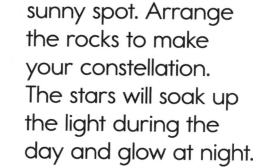

TALK ABOUT IT!
When it's dark, look up at the sky. Tell about the stars you see.

Need or Want?

People need food, water, and shelter, such as a house or apartment.

Look at the pictures. Circle each thing that people need. Draw an X over each thing that people may want, but do not need.

A need is something you *must have* to live and grow. A want is something you *would like to have* but can live without.

toys

computer, cell phone

food

water

bicycle

a place to live

TALK ABOUT IT!

How do you decide what you need?

What would happen if you did not get what you need?

What would happen if you did not get what you want?

Meeting Needs

How do people and animals meet their needs? Draw a line to match each person with an animal who is meeting the same need.

People and animals have the same needs. They all need food, water, and shelter.

TALK ABOUT IT!

How do you get the food and water you need?
How do you think animals get food and water?

Investigate:
What Do Animals Need?

Scientists observe animals in the wild. They study how animals live and grow. You can be an animal scientist, too!

> **YOU NEED:**
> • **drawing paper or a notebook** • **crayons or markers**

1. Take a walk near your home. Look for birds, squirrels, rabbits, and other animals. Watch what they do, eat, and drink. See where they find shelter.

   BE SAFE! Don't go near a wild animal or try to touch it. Observe all animals from a safe distance.

2. Draw pictures of the animals. Show how they meet their needs. Label each picture. Tell about what you observed.

3. Share your drawings with others.

chipmunk eating

bird in a tree

> **TALK ABOUT IT!**
> What did you learn about the wild animals near your home? How do you think they meet their needs?

In the Garden

This girl and her grandmother are taking care of plants. What are they doing to help them grow?

Plants must meet their needs to live and grow. Plants need light, air, water, and soil.

Find and circle at least **10** differences between the pictures below.

TALK ABOUT IT!

Do you think the plants in these pictures have what they need to grow? How do you know?

City Garden

A plant that does not get enough water or light may dry out and turn brown.

Compare these 2 plants.

TALK ABOUT IT!

Which plant is getting what it needs? Which one is not? How do you know?

Find the **8** objects in this Hidden Pictures puzzle.

pliers

teacup

banana

heart

seashell

ring

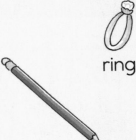
pencil

candle

Life Science: Needs of Living Things

Our Habitat, Our Home

A **habitat** is a place where living things can get what they need. Draw a line to match each animal to the habitat where it lives.

TALK ABOUT IT!

Think about where you live. Do you live near an ocean, a desert, or a forest? What kinds of animals live there?

Plant Parts

Look at this plant. Point to each part.

Many plants sprout from seeds. The roots grow down in the ground. The stems shoot up. Leaves grow from the stem.

leaf

stem

seed

root

Some plants grow flowers. Trace the lines from the flowers to the soil to show the stems.

TALK ABOUT IT!
What plants have you seen near your home?

Investigate:
How Plants Take in Water

You can use food coloring to see how water moves through a plant.

> **YOU NEED:**
> - 2 cabbage leaves
> - 2 glass jars
> - food coloring (2 colors)
> - water

1. Add water to each jar so it is three-quarters full.

2. Add a few drops of food coloring to each jar. Use a different color in each one.

3. Put a cabbage leaf into each jar.

4. Look at the leaves every hour or so.

A plant's stem is like a pipe. It moves water and nutrients from the roots to the leaves.

TALK ABOUT IT!
What happens to the cabbage leaves?
What happens to the colored water?
Why do you think these changes happen?

I Have Two . . .

Say this action rhyme.

I have two hands, **clap, clap**.
I have two elbows, **tap, tap**.
I have two ears, **wiggle, wiggle**.
I have two eyes, **blink, blink**.
I have two knees, **knock, knock**.
I have two feet, **click, click**.
But I have only one nose—**SQUISH!**

Animal Bodies

What body parts help this giraffe reach leaves? Circle them.

What body parts help this bird fly? Circle them.

Think of another animal. Draw a picture to show how it uses its body parts to stay alive.

TALK ABOUT IT!

What animal did you draw? Point out its body parts. How do its body parts help it stay alive?

Growing Plants

Put these pictures in order to show how tomato plants grow. Use **1**, **2**, and **3** to show the order.

TALK ABOUT IT!

How do you know what happens first, next, and last?

How do tomato plants change as they grow?

Draw a picture of a plant you would like to grow.

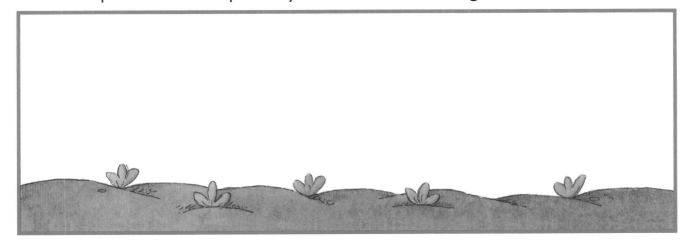

Create:
Oak Tree Models

An oak seedling sprouts from an acorn. After many years, it may grow into a tall oak tree.

oak seedling

adult oak tree and acorn

YOU NEED:

- construction paper • craft materials, such as chenille sticks, tissue paper, crayons, markers • glue or tape

1. Use craft materials to make models of the seedling and the adult tree. Be creative!

2. Glue or tape your models to the paper.

3. Share your models. Tell about the plants.

TALK ABOUT IT!

How are the seedling and the adult tree alike? How are they different?

Baby Animals

Look at this mother cat with her kittens. How are they alike? How are they different?

Young animals grow to look like their parents.

Draw a line to match each adult animal to its young.

sheep ○

○ hatchling

fish ○

○ calf

turtle ○

○ kit

fox ○

○ lamb

giraffe ○

○ fry

TALK ABOUT IT!
How are you like your parents? How are you different?

Where's the Mama?

This llama needs his mama! Can you help the baby llama find a path to his mama?

FINISH

START

Help the mama duck count her ducklings! How many ducklings does she have?

TALK ABOUT IT!
How are the ducklings like the mama duck? How are they different?

 **Create:**

Clay Animals

Make models of an adult animal and its young.

YOU NEED:
- pictures of an animal and its young
- modeling clay or play dough
- craft tools, such as shape cutters and a plastic knife for cutting dough

1. Look at pictures of your animals to help you make your models.
2. Mold the clay into one adult animal and its young.
3. Share your models. Tell about the animal and its young.

TALK ABOUT IT!
How are the adult animal and the baby animal alike? How are they different? How do your models show these ideas?

Join the Band!

Instruments make different **sounds**. How can you play an instrument?

You can use sticks or your hands to beat a drum.

 You can blow air into a trumpet.

You can strum the strings of a guitar.

Point to each instrument in the picture. Then, find and circle the **5** hidden objects.

flowerpot   spool of thread

envelope   apple

kite

TALK ABOUT IT!

Which instruments in the picture are played like a drum?

What are the children doing to play the violins?

Music Shop

A piano has strings inside. When you hit the keys, the strings **vibrate**, or move quickly. This creates sound.

Circle each instrument that has strings.

What silly things do you see?

Finish the Instruments

Connect the dots from **1** to **12** to see what instrument the man is playing. How is he playing it?

Use crayons or markers to decorate this toy xylophone.

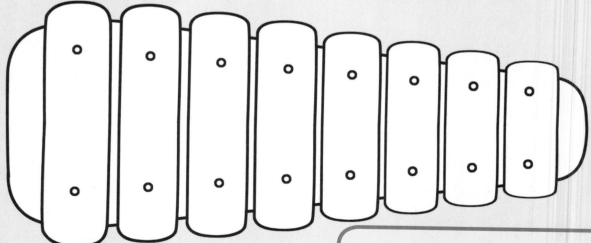

TALK ABOUT IT!
What instrument would you like to play? Tell how you would play it.

Investigate:
Your Own Drum Set

Add more cups to make more music.

YOU NEED:

- scissors • 2 large paper cups • 2 small paper cups
- markers • glue • cardboard • plastic spoons

1. Cut off the top of 1 large cup and 1 small cup.

2. Decorate each cup.

3. Glue the cups to the cardboard. Let them dry.

4. Tap the rim of each cup with the spoons. What do you hear?

TALK ABOUT IT!

What did the cups sound like? Did all the cups sound the same or did each one sound different?

Homemade Instruments

Shoebox Guitar

> **YOU NEED:**
> • shoebox   • 3 rubber bands   • 2 pencils

Adult: Cut a circle in the top of the box.

1. Place the rubber bands around the box lengthwise.
2. Insert pencils under the rubber bands.
3. Pluck the rubber bands to make music.

Shaker Cans

> **YOU NEED:**
> • plastic containers and lids   • rice
> • masking tape   • colored paper   • stickers

1. Pour rice into each container.
2. Tape the lids shut.
3. Decorate the containers.
4. Play some music and use your shakers to play along!

> **TALK ABOUT IT!**
> What happened when you plucked the rubber bands on the box? How does the rice in the shaker make sound?

Shadows

The sun gives off light. Its light shines on Earth. When an object blocks some of the sun's light, it makes a **shadow**.

Look at the shadow of the children. What is it shaped like?

Draw lines to match each shadow with the object that made it.

> **TALK ABOUT IT!**
> How are the shadows alike? How are they different?

Create:
Shadow Puppets

> **YOU NEED:**
> • craft sticks • foam or paper shapes • clear tape
> • flashlight or adjustable reading lamp

1. Tape a craft stick to each shape.

2. Make the room dark. Then, shine the flashlight or reading lamp onto a blank wall.

3. Hold up each puppet between the light and the wall. Move your puppets and put on a show!

TALK ABOUT IT!
Move your light so it shines from the side of a puppet, above a puppet, and below a puppet. Where is the shadow each time?

Create:

Sun Prints

YOU NEED:

- dark construction paper • dried leaves, flowers, and other natural items • clear plastic wrap • rocks or other heavy objects

1. Find a sunny location outside. Place the construction paper on a flat surface there.

2. Arrange natural items on the paper.

3. Cover the paper and its items with plastic wrap. Put rocks on the corners to hold it down.

4. Leave everything outside for at least 2 days. When you return, remove the plastic and see your sun prints!

The leaves and flowers block sunlight from hitting the paper. The paper underneath them does not change.

TALK ABOUT IT!
How does sunlight change the paper around the objects?

Investigate:
Which Is Heavier?

Build a balance to compare objects around the house.

> **YOU NEED:**
> • hole punch • 2 paper or plastic cups • 2 chenille stems
> • plastic hanger with notches or hooks
> • objects to test, such as coins, crayons, and marbles

1. Make holes on both sides of each cup.

2. Put 1 end of a chenille stem through a hole and twist together. Repeat on the other side of the cup.

3. Hang a cup in the notch on each side of the hanger.

4. Place the hanger on a doorknob. Put objects into each cup. How can you tell which is heavier?

TALK ABOUT IT!
Look at the items you tested. Which items are **heaviest**? Which ones are **lightest**? How do you know?

Congratulations!

(your name)

worked hard
and finished the

Hands-On
STEAM
Learning Fun Workbook

P
PRESCHOOL

Answers

Page 3
What Should You Wear?

Page 4
A Windy Day
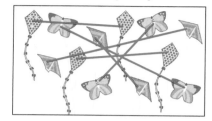

Page 13
Solid or Liquid?

Page 14
Liquids and Solids
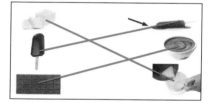

Page 15
On the Ice

Page 19
Moon Watching

Page 21
Need or Want?

Page 22
Meeting Needs

Page 24
In the Garden
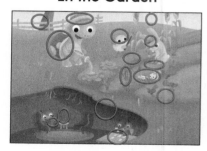

Answers

Page 25
City Garden

Page 26
Our Habitat, Our Home

Page 31
Growing Plants

Page 33
Baby Animals

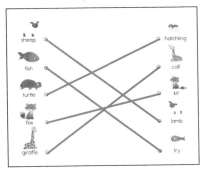

Page 34
Where's the Mama?

The mama duck has 7 ducklings.

Page 36
Join the Band!

Page 37
Music Shop

Page 38
Finish the Instruments

It's a trumpet.

Page 41
Look at Shadows

Extend the Learning

Want to explore further? Encourage your child's interest and curiosity in the topics throughout the book. Here are some ideas to get you started.

Weather (pages 2–6)

With your child, watch a weather report on the news. How is the weather described? Why is it helpful to know what the weather might be tomorrow?

Pushes and Pulls (pages 7–12)

Everything moves because of a push or a pull. Ask your child to test out toys to answer these questions: What can move each one—a push or a pull? How can you make something move faster? How can you slow it down?

Solids and Liquids (pages 13–16)

The kitchen is a great place to explore solids and liquids with your child. What solids can your child find? What are some liquids? Ask your child to look in the freezer. How do ice cubes and frozen food feel? How is this different from water and foods at room temperature?

The Sky (pages 17–20)

Go outside with your child on a clear night. Can you find the Big Dipper or the three bright stars of Orion's Belt? How does the moon look? Talk about what you see.